MAHABHARATA STORIES

The Game of Dice

Subhadra Sen Gupta

An imprint of Om Books International

As the Kauravas plotted to take away Indraprastha from the Pandavas, Shakuni said to Duryodhana, “Do you know that Yudhishthira has a weakness for gambling?”

Duryodhana laughed, “Yes! I do. He is a very bad player and always loses the game.”

Shakuni nodded with a crooked smile, “Exactly!”

Dusshasana was puzzled and asked, “Play dice with Yudhishthira? Why?”

Shakuni explained, “I will play against him and as he keeps losing I will make him wager the city of Indraprastha.”

Dusshasana was curious, “But you cannot be sure you will win.”

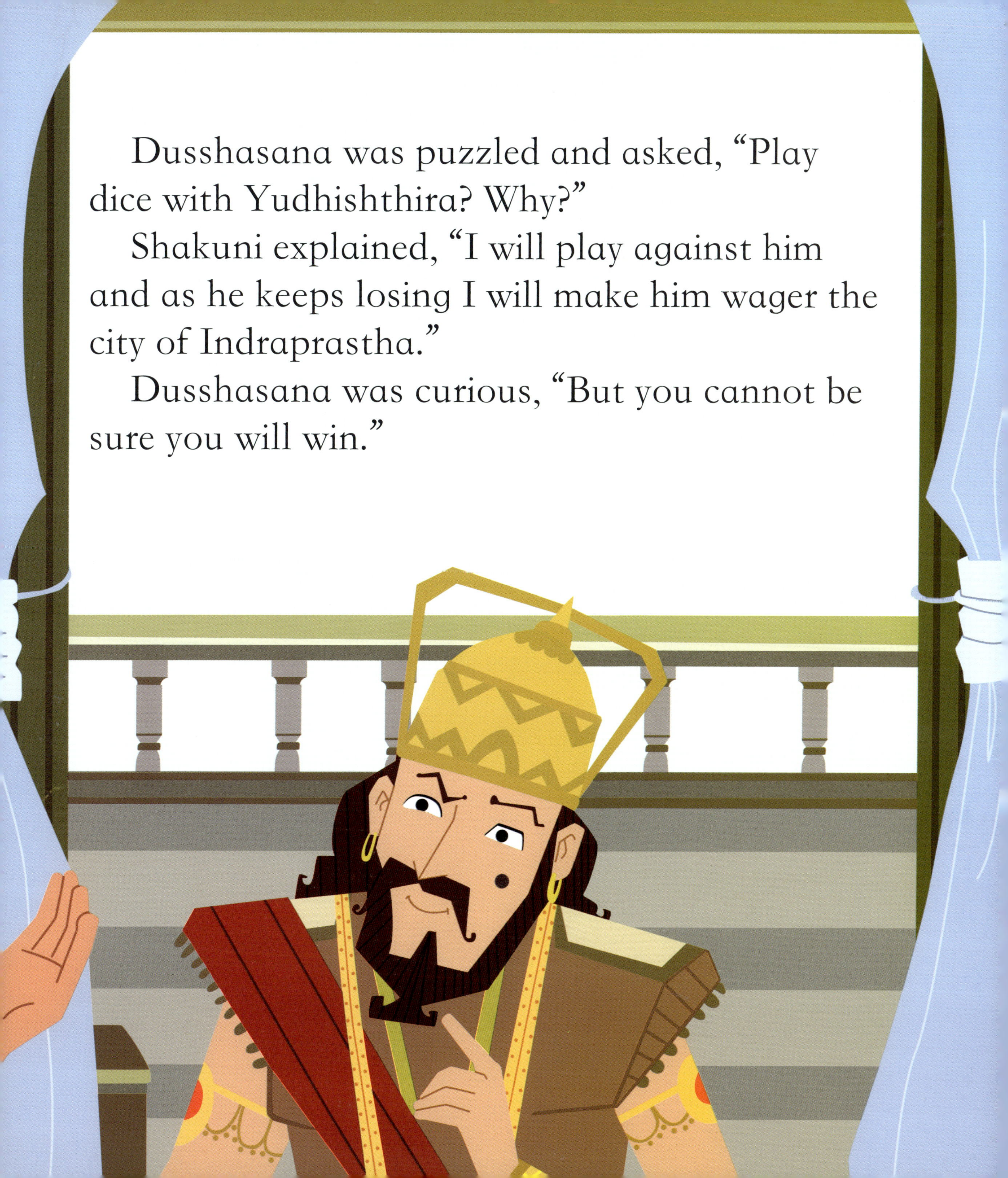

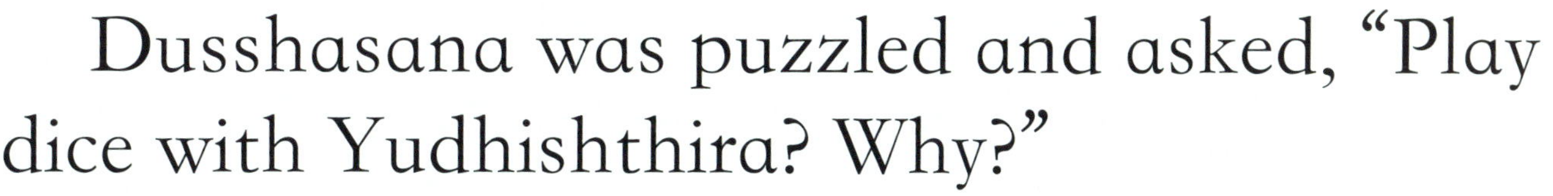

Shakuni showed Duryodhana and Dusshasana the dice he would use.

"These dice are loaded," Shakuni said. "They will fall exactly the way I want them to fall. I am sure to win."

Duryodhana invited Yudhishthira to a dice game and he accepted. The Kauravas and Pandavas gathered in the palace of Hastinapur for the occasion.

The dice game began. Shakuni played for

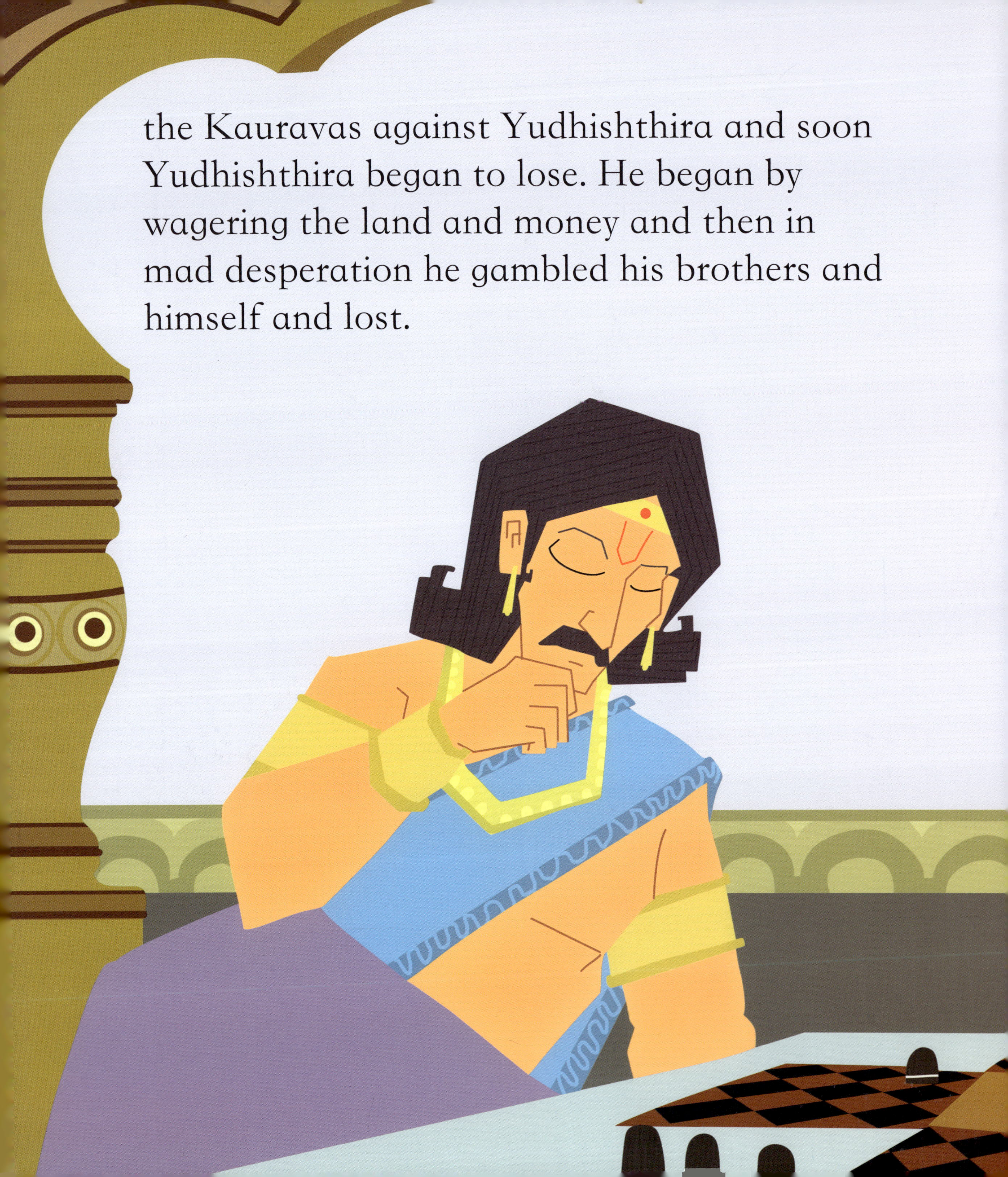

the Kauravas against Yudhishthira and soon Yudhishthira began to lose. He began by wagering the land and money and then in mad desperation he gambled his brothers and himself and lost.

Shakuni laughed at Yudhishthira and said, "You have lost everything! You are a king without a kingdom, Yudhishthira! What will you gamble next?"

To everyone's bewilderment Yudhishthira said, "I now wager my queen, Draupadi!"

Despite protests from the spectators, Yudhishthira wagered Draupadi and once again lost the dice game. Duryodhana gave a triumphant laugh and shouted, "Draupadi now belongs to me! Dusshasana bring her here!"

Dusshasana came back dragging a weeping Draupadi by her hair into the hall. To her dismay, the men – the Kauravas, Pandavas, Bhishma, Dhritarashtra – just watched helplessly and did not come to her aid.

Humiliated, Draupadi was left all alone to fight including by her five husbands. The evil Dusshasana began to disrobe her. She called out to Lord Krishna for help and prayed, "Oh Lord Krishna, help me please!"

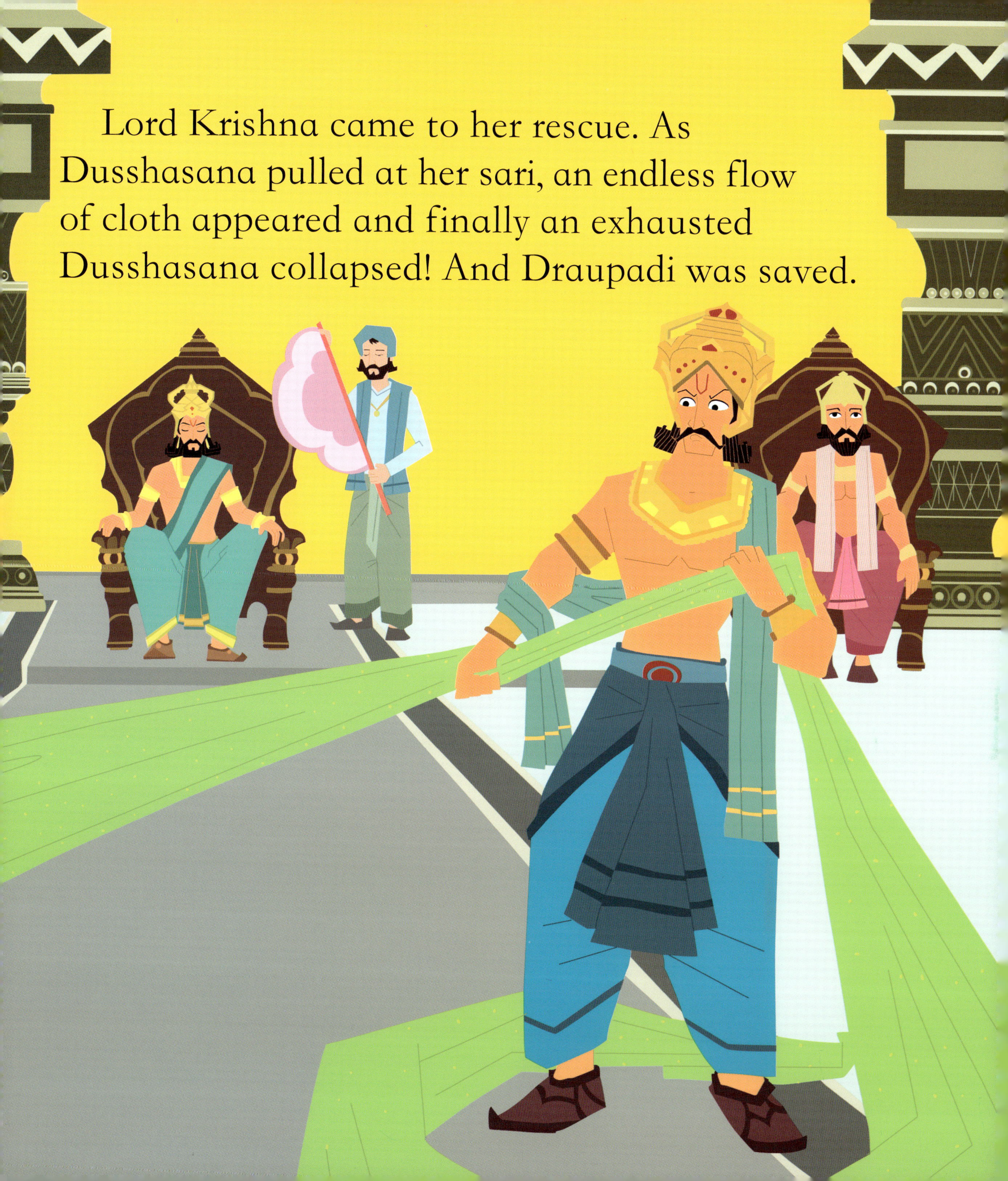

Lord Krishna came to her rescue. As Dusshasana pulled at her sari, an endless flow of cloth appeared and finally an exhausted Dusshasana collapsed! And Draupadi was saved.

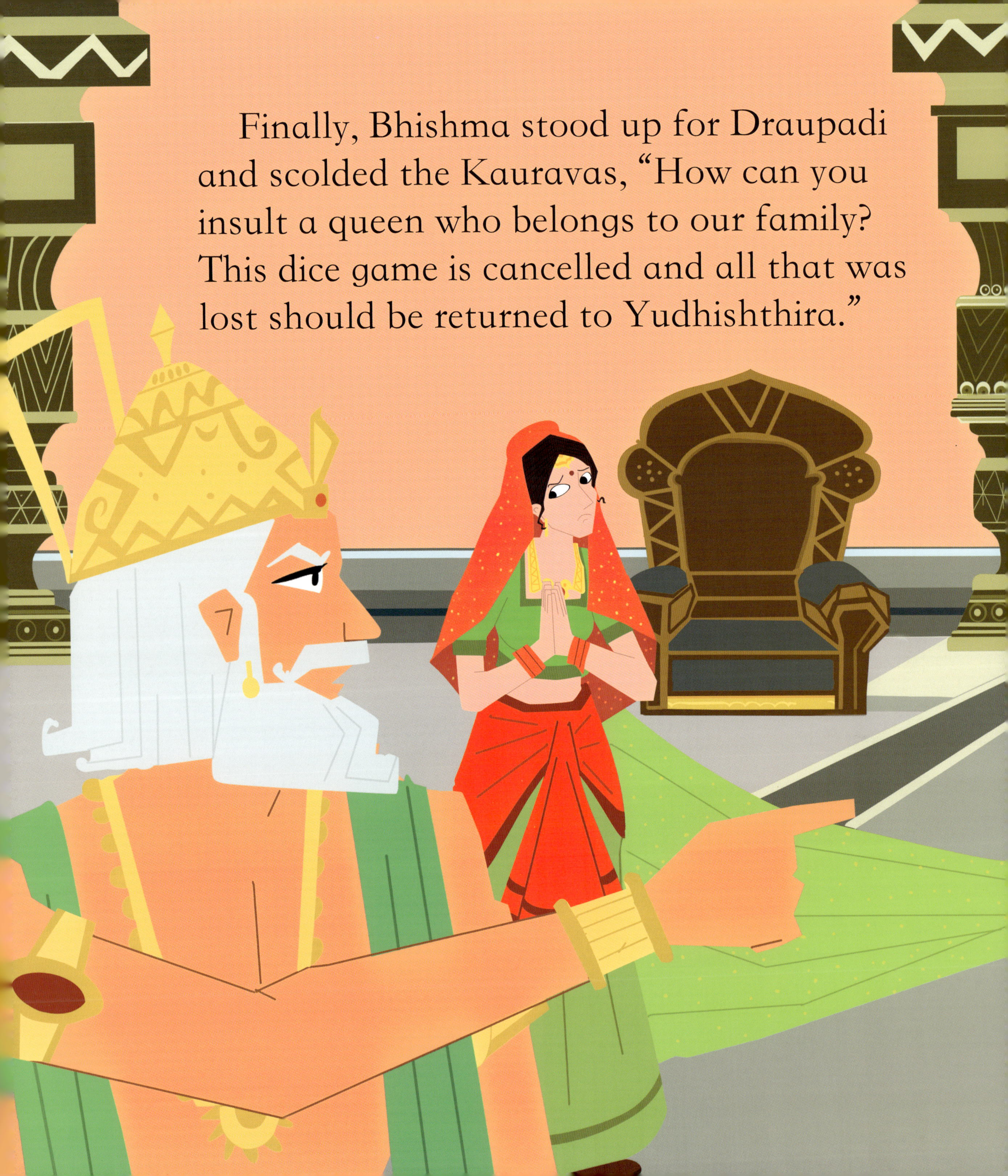

Finally, Bhishma stood up for Draupadi and scolded the Kauravas, "How can you insult a queen who belongs to our family? This dice game is cancelled and all that was lost should be returned to Yudhishthira."

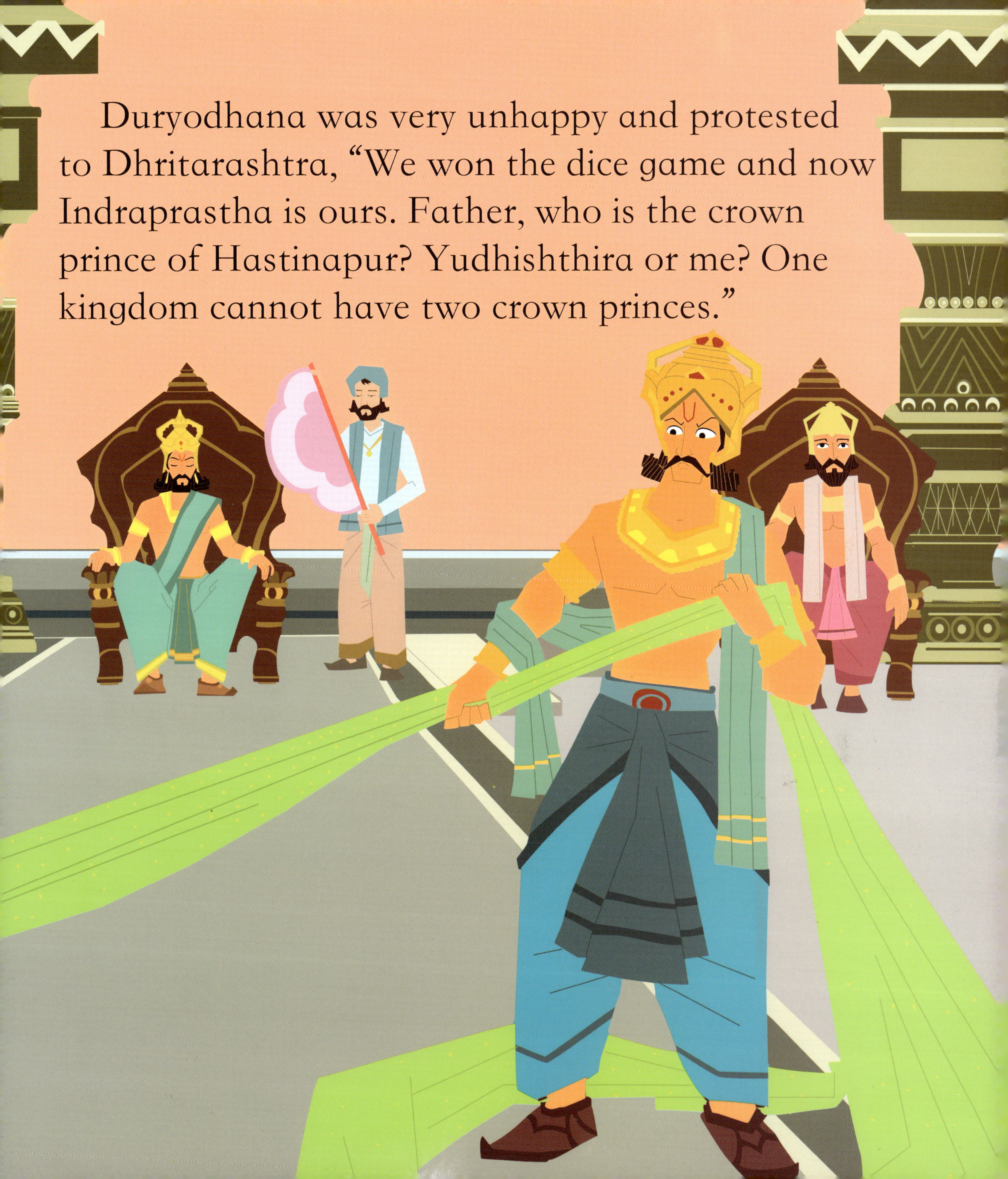

Duryodhana was very unhappy and protested to Dhritarashtra, "We won the dice game and now Indraprastha is ours. Father, who is the crown prince of Hastinapur? Yudhishthira or me? One kingdom cannot have two crown princes."

Dhritarashtra was very unhappy at Bhishma cancelling the earlier dice game. He decided that Yudhishthira had to be fooled again. He told Duryodhana, "Invite the Pandavas again for another dice game and once again make sure Shakuni defeats them."

The second invitation arrived at Indraprastha and to the shock of his brothers and Draupadi, Yudhishthira accepted the invitation and once again he lost the game.

Dhritarashtra then decided, "The Pandavas will have to go into exile for twelve years. In the thirteenth year they will have to live in hiding. If they are found they will go into another twelve years of exile." The Pandavas and Draupadi left Indraprastha and headed for exile into the forest.